TURNING ON THE LIGHT

Tips, Tricks, and Stories for Better Living with Low Vision

MS. JORDAN HANCOCK

Assisted by: Steve Neuendorf

BALBOA.
PRESS

A DIVISION OF HAY HOUSE

Balboa Press books may be ordered through booksellers or by contacting:

Balboa Press
A Division of Hay House
1663 Liberty Drive
Bloomington, IN 47403
www.balboapress.com
1 (877) 407-4847

Because of the dynamic nature of the Internet, any web addresses or links contained in this book may have changed since publication and may no longer be valid. The views expressed in this work are solely those of the author and do not necessarily reflect the views of the publisher, and the publisher hereby disclaims any responsibility for them.

The author of this book does not dispense medical advice or prescribe the use of any technique as a form of treatment for physical, emotional, or medical problems without the advice of a physician, either directly or indirectly. The intent of the author is only to offer information of a general nature to help you in your quest for emotional and spiritual well-being. In the event you use any of the information in this book for yourself, which is your constitutional right, the author and the publisher assume no responsibility for your actions.

This book is a work of non-fiction. Unless otherwise noted, the author and the publisher make no explicit guarantees as to the accuracy of the information contained in this book and in some cases, names of people and places have been altered to protect their privacy.

Any people depicted in stock imagery provided by Getty Images are models, and such images are being used for illustrative purposes only.
Certain stock imagery © Getty Images.

Print information available on the last page.

ISBN: 978-1-9822-2648-0 (sc)
ISBN: 978-1-9822-2650-3 (hc)
ISBN: 978-1-9822-2649-7 (e)

Library of Congress Control Number: 2019904560

Balboa Press rev. date: 06/03/2019

CONTENTS

MEDICAL DISCLAIMER

The information provided in this publication is not intended to replace consultation, evaluation, services, or establishment of a licensed practitioner-patient relationship. It is not diagnostic and does not replace an in-person examination and agreed-upon course of action. It is not being used, or to be implied, as a means of practicing outside of state or scope of licensure. The material is meant for information and possible supplementation of what your specific healthcare provider has provided. It should be reviewed with that person also.

The publisher(s) and author of this publication specifically disclaim all responsibility for any liability, loss, or risk, personal or otherwise, that is incurred as a result, directly or indirectly, of the use and application of any material in this publication.

To those of us who are having daily struggles with low vision—and to those persons who have the faith and the courage to overcome those obstacles.

Special thanks to Ariel Echevarria and Ariel-View Caricatures & Illustrations for the author picture, David R Haslam for his assistance in getting us started, and to Cheryl Savage for her invaluable and continued help and support.

INTRODUCTION

I am beyond belief. *No way,* I told myself. *No way am I having vision problems. I just need to rest my eyes and I'll be able to see clearly again.*

Maybe I just need more light. Maybe that TV is getting old; it's blurry. Everything is fuzzy. My eyes get tired and burn. I can't see the price tags at the market.

I'm in shock. I can't see any detail or read small print. My emotions are on a teeter-totter, splattered all over the place. Any little thing can set me off, making me scream, yell, and kick.

I've become aware of the depression I am sinking into as well as what it's doing to me. These angry thoughts are destroying my chances of repair and healing.

Why me? I pleaded silently.

I'm one of the good guys. Should I have been better? I can be a better person. I'll give more to the poor. I'll be kinder. I'll say extra prayers. I'll even be nicer to my son-in-law. I'll do anything. Just give me back my sight, even just half of it, I cried internally.

My vision fades even more. Will I go totally blind? Surely I'll be able to see movement and colors. Will I?

I am losing so much more than just my sight. I am losing my ability to function independently.

Now I'm grieving. I am seriously down in the dumps. Life as I knew it is over. Sayonara. Adios, cruel world. I bid you adieu. How far down is down? My sense of self-worth has sunk to feelings and thoughts I've never had before.

Where do I go from here? Do I tell my family? My husband? My daughters, my sisters and brothers, my friends? Or will they just think I'm a complaining old woman? It just all came on so fast.

I need to go to my inner place of "What is the worst thing that can happen?" If I can handle the worst, then the rest is a piece of cake. I refuse to be the next wilting flower.

How will I walk into a restaurant without making a fool of myself? Will I walk into the tables or bump into other people? How can I read a menu, much less sign the bill? Maybe I can get some glasses.

How will I function? I can't drive any longer, but maybe I can hire a chauffeur to take me here and there, helping me stay active.

I started asking myself the hard questions. Maybe there was help. There must be ways to meet my daily needs.

After working through a roller coaster ride of emotions and finally coming to terms with reality, I began to center myself on action. I moved into acceptance of my situation. I began to focus on solutions and looked for answers to make me normal again. I think back to advice my mom gave: "Everything is in divine order just the way it is and just the way it isn't."

Our journey on Earth would be over if we had nothing left to learn, nothing left to do. Just like the old soldier, we would fade away. Through this journey, I have become a master builder. I build my own solutions to the problems I face. I have found the tools by the simple act of "turning on the light."

I have grieved over the sight challenges that I will face for the rest of my life. *Turning on the Light* reveals a few personal stories and illuminates tips and tricks I've learned over the many years of study and learning.

Insight by insight, take my hand and we'll take a trip through the kitchen, the bathroom, the clothes closet, and the jewelry box. From food organization to travel, shopping, and other daily doings, I will make you feel more comfortable, safe, and secure in your place.

Most of us try to be as good as we can be. It takes time, concentration, and practice to change.

FRUSTRATED

Today I sit at my kitchen table. I have purchased fifteen black markers and tablets. I feel so frustrated. I want to share so much with you about being visually impaired and the resultant ramifications.

I think back to when I first became impaired. It was instant, with no warning. I decided to have my eyes checked because small print was so hard to read. I went in to do so. My husband, Gary, went with me. They told me they would dilate my eyes and that driving was not recommended. I was told my eyes would return to normal that afternoon, but they didn't. I waited until the next morning, and they still didn't return to normal. That afternoon, I became quite concerned.

The next morning, I could not see anything but a blur.

The third day, we returned to the doctor. I remember people coming out into the waiting room and taking pictures. "What's that for?" I asked. There was no answer.

They led me back into a chair and looked at my eyes and said, "You'll be okay" We were told to go home, which we did. And I was not OK, and I did not get better . . .

That was fifteen years ago. My vision is still fuzzy and blurred and my perception is off. Doctors tell me I have (age-related) macular degeneration (AMD). So, I went stubbornly into the Southern Arizona Association for the Visually Impaired (SAAVI).

Tucson is a great town. Not only does it host an acknowledged college, but it also has a huge Veterans Administration center and SAAVI, a state-run school for the visually impaired.

It was close to the holidays when my husband gently took me to the school. There was only one other woman and me. Both our husbands stood behind us in a classroom. They stared at each other across the room. The door quickly opened, and in came a woman who said, "My name is Lynn, and I have one thing to say: you will never go totally blind—never. With that out of the way, let's get down to work." I looked at the other woman across from me, and we both began to cry. I had no idea that these thoughts were so shallow in my subconscious.

School was a blessing, and I took every class that became available. Our husbands became fast friends they had so much in common. The other woman was Fran, and she and I are still friends. After graduation, I decided to stay on and share with others all I had learned for healing and knowledge. It was amazing to see college students come to SAAVI with their dogs.

I was taking a typing class, and my instructor stopped my hands by putting her hands on mine. She asked me, "Jordan, what does the color blue look like?"

Home Alone

This is the hardest subject to talk about because your needs are so different from the needs of others. So much depends on your way of life.

Whether you live by yourself, with one or more companions, or in a group/community setting, losing your sight will change the way you interact with the whole world, with the others around you, and the way everything interacts with you. Being home alone can be either devastating or super depressing—or it can be a new adventure and growth opportunity. Your choice.

Find a hobby. Build birdhouses, paint pictures, raise songbirds, host church groups, paint a neighbor's house, create a neighborhood watch ... Just do something creative. With your own imagination and ideas, the list can go on and on.

The most detrimental feeling we can harbor is that we are a burden to our family or friends. To avoid or overcome this takes lots of courage, with many smiles needed.

I understand that people today don't get to know their neighbors, but I am of the generation and opinion that it's okay to have neighbors as friends. I make it a point to get to know the families and have a cup of coffee occasionally.

When being home alone really gets challenging, this is the time to be imaginative, have fun and make this great time.

My best memory was when I invited four neighborhood six-year-olds to my patio. I put out eyebrow pencils, rouge, lipstick, and mirrors. You can find children's makeup kits in toy stores. With fun and giggles, the little girls made up one another, and they even made me up. Then came the exciting part. I brought out old hats, gloves, and boas. We all had a tea party. I was not home alone if I created a party right here in my house. This is the time to use your imagination and create fun. What could be more entertaining than having an old-fashioned tea party? Learn to play again as you did as a child.

You gentlemen can use this idea too when home alone? You probably suffer more, even though you may live with your wife, family, or others. I suggest this list of things to do when you have the boys over. You could raise goldfish or hamsters, disassemble a drill or other tool, clean and repair the tool, get the neighborhood kids to cut your grass, learn how to dance the tango, rumba, twist, jitterbug, or something else. Learn how to cover a wall in artificial brick (measure twice and glue once), practice your manners (such as opening doors), honor your parents like The Good Book tells us, have young people teach you tips and tricks on the Internet, have a ball game (you could be the catcher or the umpire), or write a book (like me). Just "turn on your light."

Don't forget you create your own reality. We can be happy and glad or ugly and sad. The choice is yours.

Keep it simple, sweetie.

GARDENING

Gardening is another great hobby that is well suited for the visually impaired. One side benefit of gardening is that in addition to its being a great pastime, you can produce things you can eat, or to decorate your house, or to give away to others.

If you're growing vegetables, remember to plant a row for yourself and one for the bugs and one for the bunnies. I hope that you will get your fair share.

My favorite gardening story is happening right now on my patio. I have a huge flowerpot, and I've planted morning glories in it for many years. This year I was delighted when all the little green leaves broke the soil. I got out my climbing fence and watered them every day. I tied string on my wire fence so they would have lots of room to grow. I fertilized them every two weeks, tied them up, and even talked to them. I told my morning glories how beautiful they were when they bloomed their deep lovely blue.

My daughter came to see my huge green plant. I asked her if her morning glories had bloomed yet. I thought mine were a little late—huge and healthy but late. "Mom, these are mostly all weeds." See, I'll just enjoy them anyhow.

Wear gardening goggles and gloves!

OUT AND ABOUT

You probably do not want to spend all of your time at home. Plenty of times, you will choose to, or even have to, go out.

Many places have public transportation systems that provide accommodation for those with handicaps. Even if you are not right next to public transportation stations or stops, many public transportation systems also provide "paratransit systems" that will take you to and from the stations or stops to your home or destination. These paratransit services are authorized by the Americans with Disabilities Act (ADA) and are available in most areas with well-established public transportation. Even in areas where public transportation is not well established, the ADA as well as public and private organizations may have transportation opportunities to assist visually impaired travelers.

Besides public transportation, you can call taxis or ride-sharing services. Friends and family can perhaps take turns delivering you here or there. It is always helpful to have someone with you when you are out anyway.

Through senior citizen centers, transportation is sometimes provided for free or at a low cost. In addition, they take medical appointments as a priority. It certainly beats walking or hitchhiking. Note that you may have to book in advance.

Cash is also a consideration. When we weigh the cost of owning and maintaining a car and paying for gasoline, tires, and insurance, the cost of hiring a companion with a car is more affordable.

Kitchen

The kitchen has always been the heart of a home. For generations, it's been where family and friends have gathered to eat dinner after church and where they gather every holiday. It's a place where women showed off their prizewinning yummy potluck dishes and the men discussed how best to grill hamburgers and hot dogs, as the football game droned on in the background. Potato salad, corn on the cob, and cookies, cakes, and pies were in abundance. As we all ate, the conversation flowed. The good and bad were passed along about every family member, and plans were made for the next gathering.

Today, as I stand in the middle of my small kitchen, I have to smile at how lucky I am. I now wear that elusive chef's tall white hat. I am independent in the kitchen by using a few basic organization skills I have learned over time. I am able to put my hands on just about anything and everything in my kitchen. The countertop lamps turn on with a touch. I am confident with my every morning beeline run toward a cup of coffee, to my using my organized drawers and cupboards.

"Don't anybody move anything. Leave it exactly where you found it, for if you move it, it screws me up big time."

Put away your own groceries so you know where they are. Before I put the cartons and bags away, I mark over the label using a heavy black permanent marker. Mark any container where the label is unclear. Write with big bold letters. In my fridge, drink boxes like almond milk, orange juice, and other juice bottles have readable labels.

A heavy marking pen and masking tape are useful tools. Mark everything. I mark boxes, bags, canned goods, and everything else as soon as it enters my space. I even use masking tape on my freezer baggies because writing directly on the bag will smudge and wear off.

My refrigerator/freezer is well organized. I consistently put things in the same place, so I don't have to search. Just about everything is in baskets, so I can take them out into the light to read the labels. No matter what needs to be frozen, it goes into a freezer bag. The food should be adjusted so it can freeze flat. After the food is frozen, place the baggies upright or lying down in a basket. In the bottom drawer is my hidden stash of chocolate covered mints, caramel, cremes, hard and soft candy, and chocolate covered candy bars. Don't tell anyone.

I like to use gas stoves because I can see the flame. When you turn off the stove, the knob will bounce up and down.

I have a microwave convection oven glued with buttons for on and off and two minutes, five minutes, and eight minutes.

To make sure I'm using the correct settings, I use many charts. I have a large chart for my microwave with the layout of the controls and readable labels, and there is one for my toaster oven. These charts can assist me in operating these tools. I placed the charts in a protective sleeve and put a bright colored ribbon in the binder hole so I can easily find my charts and identify which is for which appliance.

Contrast, contrast, contrast. I use contrasting dishes when making meals. I pick hand towels that are an opposite color and contrast with the countertops.

Though I am not a big coffee drinker, I have a coffee maker where you just put in a pod, close the lid, and push a button.

My kitchen drawers are tidy and organized. I use a ton of baskets, which you can pick up cheap at your local dollar store. Forks, knives, spoons, and bigger spoons are separated in baskets and trays, with an additional basket for straws on the side. With our misperception about our perception, use a straw in your coffee cup, milk glass, or lemonade carton, not necessary in a beer bottle. I use old tissue boxes to store plastic bags from the grocery store.

If I were to make a change, I would have kept the how-to manuals, the warranties, and the price I paid for all my appliances and the dates they were purchased, all in a kitchen binder. It's always fun to remember what my thirty-year-old pots and pans cost back then.

I am special in the fact that I am not allowed to do dishes. No matter how hard I try, it seems I am told my dishes are not clean. I have been accused of leaving a little bit of this and a little bit of that on dishes so I could get out of the chore. Not so. I truly soap and rinse the dishes.

I clean up as I work in the kitchen. I have always done the dishes, so my sink is clean and ready for the next day, before I go to bed. I also lay out all my vitamins and other needs for the next day.

I check the garbage to see if it needs fresh bags. I have and use a disposal to reduce the amount of garbage going into the can.

In my kitchen, I have very few dishes for my everyday use. I have two coffee cups, one lined with white enamel and one with dark blue inside the cup.

I have two large soup-sized bowls for everyday meals, also with one white inside and one dark. I hope I have stressed the point of how necessary contrast is for easier use and our identification for our touch, hearing, and seeing.

My mother used to have a sign on one kitchen wall that read, "We've got to get organized." On the opposite wall, another sign read, "Now that we're organized, what in the hell do we do?"

COOKING

For many people, cooking is relaxing and creative. It's like painting a picture, a work of art. In my picture, the dishes are already done.

Cooking is fun, and every one of us has some family members or friends who request their favorite dish that we make.

My sister had all of her children as guests for a few days during the holidays. We all flew in from all parts of the country. She announced that each of us would be responsible for one meal of the day. All the men drew a name. My nephew Tyler got mine. So off to the supermarket we went. He was my eyes, and I was the culinary expert. We'd pulled breakfast as our meal, and since there was a contest for the best-cooked meal of the day, we put our heads together to come up with the greatest. My question was, what the heck can be done with breakfast for a prizewinning meal?

We won second place and I got to know Tyler much better. Spaghetti and meatballs won first. A second-place finish was great. Our breakfast was French toast soaked overnight in whipped eggs, with pumpkin pie spice and lots of cinnamon, and served with bacon and ham.

Sitting at my sister's table meant you had to deposit your cell phone in a basket at the end of the table. Cooking and mealtime can contribute to great family oneness.

When it comes to kitchen creations, the hardest part for me is remembering what I already added. Even the greatest chefs can forget what ingredients they already added to the mix. Therefore, I have some tips that help me both see and know what I already put in the meal.

Everyone, not just those of us who are visually impaired, can benefit from being organized. These tricks can help everyone conquer each day and live a more organized and happy life.

Put all of your ingredients, tools, spices, and hand towels on your right side. As you use the ingredients, put them on the left side of your sink or counter.

To season your special home-cooked dish, put salt, pepper, and all spices in your hand and then add to your dish. That way you won't over spice or lose the cap in your yummy dish.

When pouring anything, put your fingers on both sides of the cup so you can feel when the cup is almost full. Hug your cup with both hands, with the tips of your fingers around the top. I use a white cup to contrast my coffee so I can see how full my cup is. This white cup can be used with cocoa, tea, and juices of all kinds. You can use dark colored cups for white and light-colored liquids. You can also buy measuring cups and spoons with different colors for each amount. Also, for liquids such as extracts or sauces or even horseradish, pour into the cap to see how much you're using. My Dad would say if you taste a spoonful of horseradish sauce, you can see a mile away.

One of the most important things we must do is take care of ourselves. When cutting anything, tuck those fingers under.

With bread, use your knife as a cutting gauge. Slide the blade up the end of the loaf and then move the blade in to the thickness of the slice you want and go for it.

Apples, pears, and fruits can be sliced in a similar fashion. It is usually best to grab the item with your fingers from the top, forming an arch with your hand, and then cutting down, slice the fruit in half. Lay each half on the flat side. Then slide your knife up the face of the item where you are slicing, bring the blade in to the thickness you want for the slice, and then slice down. (Again, don't forget to keep your fingers tucked in.)

Use masking tape around your canned goods and mark them. Mark your Jell-O, pudding, cake mixes, and microwave dinners with cooking times or necessary added ingredients. For example, for Jell-O, write one cup of cold water and one cup of hot water on the package. Easy does it.

Take all your confections, raisins, coconut, sugar, flour, cookies, and chocolate chips out of the package and put them in a clear storage container. Stack containers in the cupboard two or three high and place your masking tape with the name of the item on the front of the container.

Go slow and easy. It took years for me to collect all the colors of dishes, table mats, and cutting boards. Contrast, contrast, contrast …

If you start thinking in preparation of the future and even study *Turning on the Light*, you will make the transition into the unsighted (or "touchy-feely") world with ease.

One more tip I have not talked about is replacing knives with scissors for cutting almost everything. I use scissors to cut meat, toast, some fruits, and even celery. It's just a safer habit I've gotten used to. I have three bright-handled pairs nearby. I definitely recommend this.

I like to prepare snacks in advance, easy and healthy nibbles. I have two favorites. One is my high-protein yummies. I mix raw oatmeal, almond butter, and high protein powder with all kinds of additional goodies: coconut, chocolate chips, blueberries, or dried fruits, for example. I also add coconut oil, chia seeds, and nuts. It is fun to experiment with all kinds of food. Eating two of my high-protein balls is like a full healthy meal for me. I freeze them in my marked baggies.

My second treat is buying sliced beef, turkey, or chicken. I also buy cheese sticks. I lay the meat out flat and roll up a cheese stick in. I then put them in baggies and freeze them. I know I am eating healthy nibbles while trying to keep my sugar level balanced and maintain my girlish figure.

I have three different-colored cutting boards tucked next to the microwave. I keep all my appliance charts tucked in there also. My favorite cutting board is a paper plate. No mess, no guess! I have black countertops, and white paper plates are a wonderful contrast. If I had a light countertop, I would have to find a dark wooden cutting board for the contrast I am always seeking.

Another trick is that when I am being served at a restaurant or at a gathering with friends or family, I ask that the plate be oriented so that the main entrée is at the twelve o'clock position. This makes it easier to keep track of what is what and where it is.

Oh, just let there be soup!

I had lunch out recently with a friend at a favorite restaurant. I always ask for several napkins because with my diminished sight, I often spill food down the front of my blouse. She went and got a plastic carryout bag, cut the handles, and made a bib for me by tying the handles around my neck. I thought this was very clever.

Clothing

Even if we can't see the appearance of other people, they can see us. The "I don't care" attitude doesn't do much for our own self-esteem. Let's love and take care of ourselves mentally, emotionally, and spiritually. Although we are vision impaired, we must honor the bodies God gave us by using good personal hygiene and giving them basic attention.

A nice thing to know is that with clothing, stripes around the body (horizontal) put on the pounds and stripes up and down (vertical) slim you down. They can be used to advantage if you need help in the chest area; wear a stripe shoulder to shoulder. A great sweater works for guys who are thin and want to look as if they work out.

You will find that your appearance will reflect how others treat you. If we always treat others with honor, so will we be treated.

My grandfather always said that your hair is your crowning glory— clean, neatly groomed, and walking tall. Oh, yes, don't forget your fingernails and don't forget to wash your belly button.

Remember, faith is our eyesight, though our glasses should be smudge-free at all times also.

Many people are surprised when I tell them I am visually impaired. It's the greatest compliment I can get when they say I don't look it. You are just as capable of this same recognition. Just because we are visually impaired doesn't mean we are incapable.

I love my clothes, as they tell who I am. I believe colors talk to me, as I am sure they will to you as you begin to listen. Before I became vision impaired, for a hobby, I used to color drape people using several shades of fabric.

Years ago, a woman named Carole Jackson wrote a book called *Color Me Beautiful*. She said to assign a season to each skin tone: winter for olive- and dark-skinned people; autumn for the light red to gold-skinned base; summer for the soft pink blue-based skin, and spring for very white-skinned people.

Using your skin tone, find your season; in the book are charts of your best colors. Only winters wear pure white; the other seasons wear beige and tan. Only winters wear black; the others wear navy blue, as black is too strong for their skin coloring. Winters wear all the pure colors, like red and blue. Autumns take the palette of all colors and add gray to them. For example, pure red worn by winters becomes brick red, yellow becomes gold, and so on. Autumns wear all the colors of the earth. Summers look great in pastel oranges, greens, and so forth, with their rosy pink tones and soft, delicate colors that bring out their beautiful eyes. Springs are so light, with peaches and cream complexions. Colors like ivory, soft lemon or light royal blue work best for springs.

To identify your dark blues and blacks, take them from your closet and outside in the sunlight to identify the different colors and then mark them. There are many shades of each color, so when matching, going outside for identification works best. When you have black or dark blue slacks, look inside the pockets, for many times they are white. Mark those pockets with your black marking pens or colored fabric paint.

When I was working with girls about thirteen to fifteen years old who were in jail, color draping and style gave them lots of confidence. You too can get to know your season. Just to know you are doing the best you can is so great. We may not see clearly what we're wearing, but we know just because we know.

When you talk about clothes and color coordinating the colors for your season, the absolute next thing to think of is shopping. I discovered retail and wholesale thrift shops when my children were young. My two girls grew faster than I could remove the price tags and hang up the clothes.

I'm a winter with an olive complexion. Knowing this, I can now head for my colors. The colors for me are all the clear ones with sharp contrast. My shopping time is cut in half or even less. No need to look at the pastels, earthy, or dull colors.

I ask the person shopping in the aisle or standing close to me to read the sizes or prices. They are all so kind and always help me. In the fitting room, I ask the attendant to look for wear or tear. I ask, "Would you buy this for your mother?" I often get egg on my face because many times the answer will be no. It's too old and either has bat-wing sleeves, out-of-date fabric, or styles that were cool in my day. Some of those new stretchy tops hug so tight. I'm glad that showing my belly button has passed out of my fashion. I refuse to let my belly button hang out, even if I washed it.

At the checkout stand, I again ask the clerk the price and to check for wear and tear. Because I love to shop so often, I personally shop for others, serving their colors and style. I can hunt for a receiver of my talents and gifts. I call this my special True-Blue Angel work, giving just for the joy of giving. Angels create miracles. Why not help them?

The darker my vision becomes, the harder it gets to see colors, much less price tags. My angel work is slowing down but not finished because I have you and you have *Turning on the Light*. Let's shine our lights as brightly today and continue doing for others as you would have them do for you. Our angel work must never end.

As previously mentioned, being visually impaired, I often dribble down the front of my attire. With my thrift, resale, and consignment store shopping, I can have a full wardrobe. My closet is full, as I find I can buy four thrift store shirts for the price of one shirt from a department store.

A big tip: take a piece of clothing to the window if you need more light. For example, is it black or navy blue? Or do two colors match?

When I was working and making good money, I did not have time to shop until I dropped.

When shopping for my colors, I can save a lot of energy and not become so scattered. Most thrift stores don't sort by size but display by colors. Prices are a real guess, as I can't see them, not even with my magnifying glass that I wear around my neck. I just gather whatever I like.

A neat tip is when your shirt, for example, is "on the run." That means I've worn it once and it can be worn again. To make it easy on me, I hang it on the hanger inside out. I can feel for the seams or tags for the on-the-run clothes. I also put them in a separate group, so I don't mix them up with the unworn clothes.

I also have my clothes in my closet coordinated by color group. On the shelves, I have clear containers that are larger than shoeboxes, and they hold many of my clothing items. Panties, bras, sport bras, PJ tops, and PJ bottoms are in these containers. Mark each box with masking tape and a marking pen. Use smaller baskets for black socks, nylons, and white socks. I usually put away all long-sleeved tops during summer but no more, as it passes in three months in the Midwest. I want to keep life as simple as I can.

I have a hanger on the back of my door for my shoes. Boots are on the top shelf of my closet. Cut your shoelaces off if they are too long or you have to tie them more than once. Do this so you don't trip. The only time you want to fall is *in love*.

Smile, walk tall, and stay in style.

BATHROOM

I love the bathroom. It's the only space I can think of that is completely private. It smells like me.

Fragrance reacts on everyone's skin differently. Some like a sweet smell; some like no smell at all. I like the clean skin smell, the "I just took a shower and I smell clean" smell. Big tip: have a friend help you choose your fragrance or aftershave/cologne.

I have used the same fragrances for over fifty-five years. They agree with me. Since we have our special sense of smell, I just love a nice-smelling person walking by. If it's a man, I want to ask him if he can drive as well as he smells.

Your shower must have three grips, one on each wall, and a rubber mat to stand on for safety. It is also nice to have a grip next to the commode.

All body washes, shampoos, and hair coloring are marked on the side of the bottle. That includes the dog's shampoo.

I have a pretty basket next to the sink. This holds deodorant, mouthwash, hand wash soap, and any other necessary item for the top of your sink. Fluffy rugs are necessary for a well-used bathroom. A talking scale is optional—if you want to know how much you weigh every day. Dangerous territory.

My favorite fragrance, so I am delectable, is in a spray bottle on a counter by the bathroom door. Here is where I also keep my eyebrows, and my jewelry and earring trays.

Oops, I almost forgot. Sometimes you have to use a bathroom other than your own, like when you're out in public. Usually there are separate restrooms for each gender, and sometimes they are only identified as to which is which by signs. If you can't see the signs, you're at a bit of a loss. As always, it's best to ask if you have any doubt. If there is no one to ask, guess and then open the door, calling out hello. If someone answers and you can guess the person's gender, you will know which one to use. If you have any doubt, just ask, "Is this the men's (or women's) room?" A growing trend is to have single occupancy unisex bathrooms with locks on the door. If the door is locked, someone is using it. If it is unlocked, just be sure to lock the door behind you when entering. Count your steps and use your hands to keep your orientation so you can find the exit door on the way out.

NAVIGATION

Lines are an important part of successfully navigating in most of the situations where we need to get around. I have always found comfort when walking in hallways. A hall is full of lines. Lines are everywhere; all you have to do is pick one and follow it. There are lines where the walls meet the floor. There are lines in tile and lines in carpet patterns. Especially out in public, lines are often added for the sole purpose of increasing visibility of features that would otherwise be a hazard if unnoticed, like the edges of stairsteps or for crosswalks.

"Trailing" is the technique of letting your arm hang down at your side, with the backs of your fingers, from knuckles to fingertips, lightly trailing against a wall while you move along. When trailing my nails along walls and following my lines, I can usually move quickly and safely. Keep in contact with the wall and let your guiding hand walk you down the hallway. Trailing will let you know if there is anything different in front of you. Trailing lightly is important because you could run your fingers into an obstruction, and you wouldn't want a jammed finger. When coming to an open door or a hallway, you will usually feel a breeze and will know if you have a right turn, a left turn, or an open doorway. Lines stop and show when you come to stairs or steps.

Zip-a-dee-do-dah! Yeah, here I come, so get out of my way.

Remember to follow the lines. Restaurant tabletops form a line, as do the chair backs. Outside, there are always lines. There's a line between the sidewalk and grass. There is a line between asphalt and the curbing. There are lines of cars and rows of lights, lines all around and up and down. Lines are there to guide us from just about anywhere to just about anywhere else.

Let the lines be your guide and your fingers be the trail guide, and your senses will take you where you want to go. Trailing helps give me a sense of my personal space and where in the world I want to walk.

I have been white cane trained. Visually impaired people have used canes as mobility tools for centuries, but it was not until after World War I that the white cane was introduced. Any cane or tool to extend your reach will help you in getting around and avoiding obstacles, but the white cane is also a clear indication to others that the user is visually impaired. The white cane has special significance for navigating around traffic, with drivers being required to recognize that the user is visually impaired and that special precautions are required.

I don't always use my cane because of the use of my peripheral vision, which usually allows me to see enough to function outside my house. I do like to use a cane when I travel. Being truthful, I will share that there have been times when I get turned around and, well, become lost, confused, and disoriented.

Once my helper at a grocery store left me abruptly, being called to the front of the store over the intercom. He left me at the back of the store in the dairy department. I panicked a bit before settling down and thinking things through. Another shopper saw my frustration and helped me get oriented toward the front door. I followed my lines to the registers and the window light. My grocery list wasn't quite filled yet, but so much time had passed that the bus driver had come in to look for me.

Another time, I was shopping at Sal's Place, our local donation center and thrift store. After filling my cart with good deals, I thought to try on a few. This particular store didn't stock clothing by size, so I needed to try them on. I'm not sure who was more surprised, him or me, when I thought I saw "wo" in the men's sign and barged into a men's dressing room. Boy, sometimes it really sucks to be visually impaired, especially because I didn't see a thing.

STAIRS

Stairs present a special challenge to the visually impaired. If using a cane, there are several actions to find the start and the base for each step and check to make sure the stair is clear.

Without a cane, steps are not an insurmountable obstacle, but do take a little extra care. Importantly, do not become "overly familiar" with stair navigation, even those in your own house or otherwise in your normal course of travels.

Keep your balance and your composure; take a deep breath and there you go.

For going downstairs, use the handrail if there is one. Lean your shoulder or hip into the wall or balusters, if there. Let the wall guide you down.

Hit the edge of the first step on the back of your heel. Slide your foot down. With your first foot at the bottom of the step, slide your other foot down. Repeat until you reach the bottom of the stairs. Be careful to anticipate turns or winding staircases. Stairways are often not well lit so be extra careful to let your feet be your guide. Hang on to the rail as you go or, if the stairs turn, trail your hand along the wall. Count your steps. You might return, and it will be safer. One step down at a time.

For going up the stairs, gently hit your toe into the next step up. Hang on to the handrail and go up one step at a time. Count stairs for making it easier and safer when you go back down or for a familiar stairway so you will know when you have reached the top. (Trust your counts but be sure to verify them.) When you reach your destination, feel the floor change to carpet or tile or whatever.

You know that life is full of ups and downs, yet you made it. Just take one step at a time.

TRAVEL

Traveling by air is a joyous adventure. I use a hard-shell suitcase with unusual designs. It's a white rolling suitcase painted with giant colorful butterflies. Something like that is hard to miss on the luggage carousel.

My reservations are called in for wheelchair assistance and a window seat. My daughter and caretaker (best daughter in the whole world) orders these things online for me. I pack quite light, as I have always packed too much in years past. Too much extra wash to bring home.

At the airport curb, they take my luggage and put me in a wheelchair. We're off. I always carry my red-and-white cane in my lap. The cane says a million words to those around me, and they make way for the wheelchair.

I zip through inspection. I don't know if it's my cane, the chair, my age, or my beautiful brown eyes, but I'm quickly parked at the airplane gate. I like to make friends with those around me, so I start up some conversations.

I wear a lanyard with a pouch with all my travel papers around my neck—my tickets, my passport and ID, my itinerary, claim checks, and tip money for the porters and attendants. Also decorating my pouch is my Rotary pin. This pin identifies me as part of 1.2 million club members that I can count on for help. I have made many friends while traveling.

Usually they take me aboard first. I feel like a special person, as the service given is so gracious. I usually give a large tip to the porters, as I have found most of them are college kids working to go to school or to support young families.

The most exciting boarding experience happened as I was leaving St. Thomas, Virgin Islands, which is south of Florida, by the way. I was rolled to the other side of the plane and onto a lift platform. Whoopee! I couldn't stop laughing. I just hung on tightly as I rose up and up to the doorway. I knew the other passengers had climbed up stairs, and I could tell they were right across from me. I'd made it.

Changing planes in Florida, we got on a tram and went to the next gate. I have always traveled alone and felt so secure with the great service and care the airlines offer.

Traveling in a car is just traveling, unless you try to drive yourself. Wear your sunglasses. Protect your eyes from UV rays.

MARKET SHOPPING

Market shopping can be a daunting challenge. Most markets, however, will usually be glad to help you spend your money with them. Go to customer service and ask for a personal shopper. Many markets now give you the ability to order your items online and you just pick them up or have them delivered. Hooray for online shopping—if you can see the computer. I do everything I can to avoid going to the market because I have to strain my eyes to see.

When I do go to the market, I come prepared with a very detailed list. Otherwise, I over shop and don't want to discard anything because of the expiration date. My list must be complete and precise, as that personal shopper is being paid by the market. I don't want to lose this gracious service. To get by the chocolate counter is a miracle in itself.

When bagging food, I like to bring my own mesh bags—refrigerated item in one, canned goods in another, and so on. This makes it easier to sort items when putting them away. As I am putting things away, I put labels on everything so I can easily identify an item when I go to use it later.

To store the market plastic bags, I use square tissue boxes. I wrap the bag around my finger and pop it in the box. I also put three or four of the bags in the garbage can for liners so I don't have to hunt for the new ones when changing garbage bags.

Take care with marking and organizing your groceries as you put them away. First in, first out. There is nothing more disgusting than finding something in your refrigerator or cupboard that is moldy, smelly, wiggles or bites. When in doubt, throw it out!

Basic Tools

There are many simple and basic tools to help cope more easily with vision impairment.

Identify everything you need by putting on readable labels.

There are several types of labels and labeling tools. Two-inch Masking tape is what I use. I like to keep two large rolls and write big and bold so I can read them.

I use bold black markers for writing my labels. I buy large packages of the sizes that best fit my needs. I use markers for everything—writing down doctor's appointments, chores for the day, my grocery list, and anything else I am supposed to remember. Rather than having to hunt for my lists, I put them on the front of the refrigerator with magnets. Can't help that I am a genius with new ideas sometimes.

Magnifying glasses are important tools too. Where you are in your scope of vision loss determines what you will need. My handheld magnifying glasses are numbered ten. They have almost outgrown their usefulness as I get older. It's like the chrysalis thinking life can't go on and then emerges from the cocoon as a majestic beautiful butterfly.

It is always helpful to have young people around. We can meet the opportunity of moving into the electronic age with the help of our children and grandchildren.

Clear storage containers are very useful. I collect them at the market when they are full of nuts and candy, and then the containers are wonderful for nuts, bolts, screws, kitchen condiments, buttons, yarn, or anything else where just glancing will let you know the contents. They can stack perfectly too.

Baskets and trays are an absolute must-have. They hold anything we would need them for and we can carry them to the light.

In the bathroom, I have before and after baskets for before and after my shower: one for toothpaste, shaving products, and the like, and one for deodorant, cologne, and so forth. Both can be taken to the light to see what is there.

I use half cut colored beads glued on my landline telephone numbers two, five, and eight. I know the phone is obsolete, but I am comfortable with it. I use the beads on my microwave and toaster oven buttons too—and anywhere else where I need to find a "home row" reference point.

Of course, a coffeepot is a must-have tool, even for the sighted.

Magnets are on the must-have tool list. They can be used to attach notes or instructions to the refrigerator, the stove, or anything metal.

Colored hand towels of contrasting colors are useful for finding them on countertops. They can also be used to organize things laid on them. For my medicines, I use a yellow hand towel to lay out my medicines and vitamins. I use a small red baggie for my morning ones, a yellow baggie for my afternoon ones, and a blue baggie for my night ones.

I find that having all sizes of freezer and sandwich bags is extremely useful too. I usually unpack my groceries, put one serving's worth in each bag, and label it. This makes it easy to put together a meal. Just find and grab one package for each item you want to include.

Multicolored measuring cups and spoons are useful tools as well. You don't have to read each one to see how much it holds. For example, the yellow one may always be one cup or one tablespoon.

Clothespins can be useful for things like closing chip bags. They come in many different colors and sizes. Sometimes I cannot even see paper clips, so clothespins are great.

Also wear sunglasses (for UV protection) whenever you are exposed to sunlight.

Have an "I can do it" attitude—all sizes.

This list will change as your world changes and grows.

Signing your name

One of the harder tasks for the vision impaired is signing one's name. We often need to sign documents or charge slips, like when we eat in a restaurant. Ask the server to put a finger on the X or wherever your signature is supposed to start and put your finger there. Sign your first name, then put your finger where you stopped signing your first name and sign your last name. Works like a charm.

It's Okay to Cuss

As we are visually impaired, our perception is totally off.

In all these years, I have not figured out whether something I "see" is really closer or farther than it appears. My balance and perception are both off.

When I walk into something out of order, it's okay to cuss.

When my shoelace wants to trip me, I cut it off.

As for setting a glass on the countertop when the countertop isn't there, it's okay to cuss.

When the cat or dog want to get under my legs, I don't cuss; we just discuss.

PERIPHERAL VISION

Understanding peripheral vision and learning how to use it has been one of the most absolutely important elements of my learning to cope with my visual impairment and "turn on the light." Had I not learned this, I doubt I would be able to see anything, as I have zero central vision.

Peripheral vision is the part of vision beyond the center of view. Peripheral vision is the largest portion of visual perception, approximately 100 degrees of normal 170-degree field of view.

Peripheral vision is described in three segments, with the edge of the field being the far peripheral vision, mid peripheral vision nearer the center of field of view, and near peripheral vision just adjacent to the center of your gaze.

Loss of peripheral vision is known as tunnel vision. The opposite condition—the loss of central vision while retaining peripheral vision—is known as central scotoma.

Age-related macular degeneration (AMD) is one of the leading causes of visual impairment and affects over six million people worldwide. AMD causes the blurring or complete loss of central vision due to damage to the area of the retina called the macula. There are different stages (early, intermediate, late) and two forms of AMD: wet and dry. Dry AMD occurs in about 90 percent of patients and is characterized by a slow progression of the disease.

The macula is a small central area in the back of our eye where we sense our clearest vision. As the macula degenerates, we only see with the light-sensing cells that are around the macula, forming our peripheral vision.

For us to turn on the light, we have to learn to "look around" our natural central vision and use our peripheral vision to focus on what we need to see from out of the corners of our eyes. Learning and practicing this is the most important advice I can offer.

Here is how I learned to do that to see people. I imagine the person's face is at the center of a large clock. By focusing the center of my vision on the imagined time numbers, I can see the person's face with my peripheral vision. My best views are when looking at five or seven o'clock. For your versatility and comfort, practice using other time positions. Without learning to use these techniques and tips with my peripheral vision I would not practically have any useful sight at all.

Be patient with yourself. Turn on your light and shine as you never have before. God said he was the light.

Nuts and Bolts

With all of today's known research and doctors and scientists predicting that there will be technology to actually correct vision problems in the not too distant future, there will be sight. Miracles never cease.

Meanwhile, while waiting for the upcoming miracles, there are a considerable number of products and devices available for the vision impaired. There are two general categories of these products: those that help you to better use your vision, like magnifiers and lights, and those that help you to better deal with your environment, like gadgets and tools.

In the first category, products that help you to better use your vision, magnifiers are at the top of the list. There are two general types of magnifiers. There are the traditional optical magnifiers in many different strengths, using a lens or lenses to enlarge an image. Many of these also have built-in lights that will brighten the image. You can wear one around your neck when you go shopping. The other main type is the video magnifiers, where a camera captures the image to be magnified and it is displayed on or projected to a screen. Some of these video magnifiers will also read text aloud or identify objects and say what the image is. Other items in this category include color identification tools that will state the color of the captured image. This category includes illumination tools, such as different types of flashlights.

The second category is the one with general tools for coping with impaired vision. These range from rather sophisticated tools like ultrasonic mobility aids (like your own radar) to handy gadgets like money sorters or sock clips to organize matching socks. This category includes traditional canes, talking clocks, and even cell phone or tablets/computers specially designed to accommodate low vision use. One of the interesting gadget types is the voice labeling system. Instead of using marking pens and masking tape, as I've described throughout this book, there are systems where you can create a label for an item by recording whatever you need the label to say and then attaching the label. When you want to read the label, scan it with the system tool and it will read it back to you. This would work well when you may want to use large marking for easy identification, along with the voice label tool for more detailed instruction that you may not be able to fit on a written label.

One versatile breakthrough type of product is called a "smart speaker." Early in the technology revolution, computers both created many new and now indispensable capabilities as well as replaced existing ones. In many ways, smart phones have proved as alternatives for or have replaced computers and older technologies, also giving us many more opportunities for the technology to make our lives more robust and convenient. One problem with most of this technology is that using them generally requires visually related physical activity, such as reading results and performing physical responses and tasks.

Smart speakers are a significant improvement in making all this technology available to the visually impaired. All of the smart speaker's function is accessed through an audio interface. Since audio is all or mostly hands-free, it is also largely vision-free. You can take notes to make lists or set reminders, with no need for pen and paper or a keyboard. You can read books and articles or listen to any type of music and news without needing to access any of the traditional media or equipment involved with these activities. You can access the wealth of information from the Internet just by asking. It can even tell you the joke of the day. Alarms, timers, reminders, or even conversations are there for the asking. These devices can also interface with other tools, so you can use the smart speaker to maintain your phone directory and initiate calls or to write and receive text messages, audible, of course. The speakers can be connected with other devices to control lights, appliances, and controls. These can also perform many important safety and well-being functions, such as communicating with emergency services and caregivers.

And of course, new products are continually being invented and made available. Make sure you have plenty of batteries to keep your electronic tools and aids working properly. No more excuses for forgetting birthdays or losing telephone numbers. Don't expect a voice command Seeing Eye dog robot anytime soon. They can't seem to solve the problem of them depositing little batteries throughout the house. Wow, what next?

BEST FRIENDS

One of the greatest gifts of living with my son-in-law and my beautiful daughter is "Joey." Joe Cocker is a soft curly buff-colored Cocker Spaniel. He is a cuddler and hugger, with freckles and the longest eyelashes you ever saw. In the middle of the night, Joey comes to nestle behind my knees or into my stomach. Sometimes he's a little smelly, but I don't care. It's only me and Chloe, my little four-pound white teacup poodle anyway.

Joey is a working dog. Ever since he was a puppy, he has gone to work with my daughter. They leave the house early in the morning. It seems Joey's internal alarm clock sends him bounding downstairs into my space. He jumps on me, licks my face and says, "Grandma, get up. I'm leaving for work. I wanted to tell you I love you. Bye."

I believe God gave us Joey and other working animals, but especially dogs and cats, to teach us about unconditional love. They show their love to you no matter what color you are, what language you speak, or how rich or poor you may be. The wag of that tail says to me hello and goodbye so perfectly. Some dogs are so highly trained that they were used in wars as both guides and hunters of our enemies. An actual bounty was put on their heads, because they were considered the perfect soldier. Today the visually impaired person's greatest gifts are those 4-legged soldiers who guide and protect us.

I have only visited a Seeing Eye dog training center once. I was amazed at the vastness of the training program. There were breeding pens where dogs could mate and have their puppies. There was a harness shop, where each dog received a proper fit of leashes, collars, and so forth. College-age kids and families were selected to receive the puppies. It was their job to teach them basic puppy manners and potty habits so they would be prepared for future intense training. When a pup reaches a certain age and has sufficient knowledge, it is brought back to school to begin Leader Dog training. Only a few select dogs will pass muster because many may find squirrels more fun to chase than leading people across a street filled with all the cacophony of noise, vehicles, and pedestrians.

After the dogs are well trained, it is now time for the visually impaired person to be trained. Typically, the visually impaired person stays in residence at the school while being trained to handle their service dog. When all is said and done, and graduation day arrives, the two lives are joined together as one. When I attended SAAVI, I was offered a guide dog, however, I turned down the offer because I had met so many high school and college aged students who had a real need of a dog. I chose to pass the gift onto someone younger and more active than myself.

It's amazing that dogs are now being trained to warn a person of an oncoming seizure. I think everyone within my circle of friends has the gift of a pet, a dog, or cat to love them. What loving gifts to humankind they are.

When I said Joey was a working dog, I meant a watchdog; a scout. He is the official welcoming committee at the door and the "Thank you. Come again.", greeter at my son-in-law and daughter's business. Any new hires must be personally introduced to Joey. My daughter takes the person by the arm, and they get to know each other. Joey must approve, "You're okay—and welcome."

Every day Joey does his inspection of every nook and corner of the warehouse; no snakes, spiders, cats, or gophers are allowed in the warehouse. You would have thought aliens had landed with all the barking and noise he made one day. He'd found a nest of small mice, and bark and whined, until every one of them was removed. Nobody could find much peace at work that day.

When my son-in-law and daughter are out for the evening, Joey becomes very protective of me. If there is any noise or movement, Joey becomes a fierce watchdog. Chloe, my poodle, finds great comfort in Joey being there too. Dogs are so smart; I often wonder if Joey knows I'm low vision.

Once I flew to my sister's in Maryland., I got special permission from my doctor and vet to have Chloe travel along as my comfort dog. Traveling with a dog friendly carrying case, I could keep my hand inside the opening, so we could comfort each other and travel nicely without anxieties. She also notifies me when danger is near or a stranger approaches. I feel so much comfort and relaxation when my dog is with me.

I cannot say enough about my love for animals. There are as many kinds of dogs as God has the imagination to create: working dogs, watchdogs, pet dogs, police dogs, way too many barking dogs, service dogs, comfort dogs, and just plain lazy dogs. For me, the most precious of all, are the guide and leader dogs. They are so highly trained and so very dependable, that we actually put our lives in their paws. Thank you, thank you, God, for these blessed animals, truly they are our best friends and they certainly "turn on the light" for me.

TELEPHONES

Yes, I have an old-fashioned landline, as mentioned. I have glued half cut colored beads on the numbers two, five, and eight. By doing this, I can find the rest of the numbers.

I have a directory sheet with all my programmed phone numbers on it, those of my daughter, dentist, friends, relatives, and several people whom I have forgotten are listed. I have a copy in my purse and on the kitchen table. I have sixty-six phone numbers. My daughter is number one, and the dentist is sixty-six. On my list, I also have my home number and address on the bottom of the page in case anyone else would need to use them, such as in an emergency.

I have an old-fashioned flip cell phone that has extra-large light-up numbers. A flashlight is built into one end for close-up reading. On this phone, and on most phones, the number five has raised bumps, and it can be found by touch. The phone has a special feature. If the number is programed into the phone, I can hit a special button and a voice will ask me whom I want to call. No excuses for not using this high-tech gadget.

Money, Money, Money

Money makes the world go around. But if you can't see it clearly, it will make your head spin around too.

I find that as I get older, my needs are less, but I still must deal with money.

I don't smoke, don't drink, and don't party in beautiful clothes. In my old-age wisdom, I have decided I will give my children the dignity to learn and earn as I did.

The saying that you can't take it with you is also great wisdom, but you still have to take some with you to go to the store or for dinner, and I can share some useful tips and tricks.

Handling cash can vary around the world. In US cash, all the bills are the same size and mostly the same color and texture. The denominations are printed in large letters on the back, so it is a little easier to tell which bill you are using. Other currencies use different sizes and colors and sometimes even textures for the different denominations. Change is a little easier since each denomination is a unique size and weight. You do need to be careful, though, that you are not mixing similar coins from different countries—like US quarters and Canadian quarters.

I find that using a folding system for handling cash is handy. Each denomination is folded differently. For example, twenty-dollar bills can be folded the long way in half. Ten-dollar bills can be folded end to end. Five-dollar bills can have one end folded on the diagonal. Leave your one-dollar bills flat. You will figure out what is comfortable for you. My daughter is in total charge of my life. She gracefully handles my money.

I am in charge of all the men. The first requirement is that they drive. The second requirement is that they bring a health certificate and a Dun & Bradstreet credit rating.

I just went to the dentist. I had to go to a specialist, and the cost was one and a half times my monthly social security income. I guess I'd better require dental clearance as part of my requirements toward males.

He either has money or doesn't—just so long as he can drive.

My job is full time because the search for my heartthrob is never ending.

Using credit cards and other alternative payment systems, such as electronic payments, can be a bit of a challenge. If you use more than one card, you want to make sure you can tell the difference between cards. If you use payment apps on your smart phone, it is probably best to learn a combination of voice and keyboard commands to assure you pay correctly.

Many banks and other financial institutions will provide the services of a financial advisor to their customers, including the advisor coming to your home if you have difficulty.

Remember to hide a hundred-dollar bill somewhere—you never know when you'll need it. While giving thanks for all I have today, I must include the one hundred dollars I have hidden. I bet no one will ever find the money, but I know it's safe because I have forgotten where I put it.

Lights, Clocks, and Tabletop

I have lights of every size and type to help me see anything I need to see. There is a large chandelier with five lights hanging over my kitchen table/office-communication center/telephone operating center/dining area, and so on.

I have two illuminated handheld magnifying glasses there too. I have two in case I can't find one fast enough.

Knowing the time is important, especially when you have commitments, appointments, and the need to keep some sort of a schedule. I have many clocks, some small and some very large. I can see the large clocks, especially because of the high-contrast white face and big black numbers and hands. The smaller clocks are talking clocks that will announce the hour. These are set a few minutes apart so that at least on the hour, I have several reminders as to what time it is. I also use timers with buzzers. I have also learned to use my smart speaker to announce the time and set alarms and timers. These are used when I have to call you back or, check on something in the oven or the washer or dryer. Two buzzers are better than one.

I always thought I would need to be buzzed for the dog to go outside, but it seems my pet has her own timer and it's more reliable and accurate than mine.

Another advantage of my large clock is that is has an audible ticktock noise that helps me feel connected with reality. It's just good for my ego.

I have my table located next to a large window—it gets even more light.

I keep a short glass full of different size black markers. I buy spiral notebooks at back-to-school sales. I purchase at least a dozen or more. Since I can't usually read my writing, I can write in huge black appointments numbers, phone numbers, and messages to myself. Not to mention my to-do list, which never gets done because I can't read it. Now who is amazing and brilliant?

Am I great at manufacturing excuses?

Medicine and Vitamins

Taking our medicine correctly is an important necessity. I use the contrast method for my daily doses of medications by laying small different color baggies on a contrasted hand towel. I use a color-coded system to separate medicines by the time of day.

Individual doses are placed in square colored baggies. My daughter helps me by measuring out all of the doses. She does it for thirty days in advance and puts the doses in the bags for me.

I use red for morning. Red is action—I have to get out of bed. Yellow is for afternoon—sunshine and ideas. Blue is for bedtime—nighttime, romance shutdown, time to be hopeful you have a dog or cat to cuddle at your feet as you sleep, and of course blue for peace and time to grow and meditate. When I am finished taking the medicine, I tuck the empty bags under the end of the towel.

EYEBALL TO EYEBALL

Look people in their eyes, at least where you think their eyes are, and smile. You may be wearing glasses, sunglasses or not, but people will become more engaged with eye contact. Get people to look right back at you eyeball to eyeball.

Referring to glasses, my timeline went something like this. In the beginning, I went to the dollar store and bought three or four pairs of reading glasses, one for every room in the house and for the patio table, all in order to read the small print that daily life is full of: the TV guide, my daily horoscope, boxes of food, and the infinitesimally small writing on pill bottles. It helped me differentiate between hemorrhoid cream and face cream and allowed me to punch those crammed little numbers on the house phone in order to call my friends. It took a year or so before I had to up the ante and get stronger drugstore glasses. I moved through all the glasses they had to offer pretty fast. I finally gave in and made an appointment with the eye doctor. The rest gets worse from there.

When I was sighted, there was nothing worse than seeing someone wearing dirty, smudgy glasses with fingerprints. I just wanted to rip them off their noses and wipe them clean. Maybe you can't see the smudges, but everyone else can. Keep your glasses cleaned as a good grooming habit.

Is it necessary to tell people you are visually impaired, or handicapped? I hate to take pity. And I certainly don't want to hear all the medical problems everyone's cousin or uncle or brother had. I'm not interested in their aunt Maddie's blindness and how terrible it was. So, do I tell them?

I usually do say something to food servers and cashiers. Most of the time, retail workers are real people persons. As you talk with them, you can pick up and feel their energies and tones of voice. Do you hear friendliness, intrigue, or are they distant? Do they have their arms crossed and are they turning away from you?

Learning to protect yourself from negativity is an art. I work on painting only positive pictures. I paint in my mind's eye. I try to look through the eyes of love and paint my world in Technicolor.

What do you call yourself, blind, low vision or a low-vision person? It's really your decision, and how people may or may not react to you is theirs. The word blind seems a much stronger word than visually impaired or low vision. People always ask the question "Are you legally blind?" I never figured exactly what "legally" meant. Either you can see enough to do a task, or you can't.

Others may not even notice that you can't see them. It might depend on how comfortable you are in the telling of it.

I did a fun test one day at church. As a greeting, I asked each man who passed me by if he was cute or ugly. He always answered ugly and laughed. I would then ask him if he wanted a blind date. We both laughed, and I had a new friend.

How to Have Stimulating Conversations in a Delicate Situation

One of the things you will likely encounter is that people will want to discuss your condition and offer advice. While they most likely mean well, it is probably not your favorite topic and they are not the best persons for knowing what is right and best for you.

Just Say "Uh-Huh"

These two words can help you get past just about any situation. Recently, I told my young driver how to use this special word, giving him some practical examples.

Let's say you pick up a fare and they talk incessantly and complain and complain. If they say something that requires a response, just say "Uh-huh."

"Can you be the designated driver?" Just say "Un-huh."

"Life is just a bowl of cherries." Just say "Un-huh."

On to the next, "Uh-huh."

Just Say "Oh"

Saying "Oh" acknowledges you are listening, but it does not let on if you are agreeing or disagreeing with the speaker. For example, if someone is gossiping, just say "Oh" at some appropriate point, and, unless you want to hear it all, take the opportunity to politely excuse yourself.

'My Aunt Maddie was blind too." Just say "Oh."

"I hear they have glasses now that you can wear and see as well as a sighted person." Just say "Oh."

"Why is it that we unsighted know so much?" Just say "Oh."

"Did you hear about the agnostic dyslexic who spent a lot of time wondering if there was a dog." Just say "Oh."

"I Hear What You're Saying"

"I think your ideas are all wrong", just say, "I hear what you're saying".

"California is going to fall into the ocean – you will need a new bikini.", just say, "I hear what you're saying".

Other people usually want to help. Don't let them mislead you. Often these words tell the other person you are acknowledging them and that their statement is heard by you without any agreement or disagreement.

How great. Practice "Uh-huh" and "Oh" and "I hear what you're saying."

With these responses, we can become the un-opinionated conversationalist and never have to say "bullsh*t."

THINGS THAT GO BUMP
IN THE NIGHT

"Bump in the night" is a reference to those things that are (or certainly seem) real to us but are considered beyond physical reality. These include spiritual and religious beliefs as well as those things that we do not fully understand or are not able to explain. Losing one's sight often results in "phantom eye syndrome," where people "see" things that aren't there (or at least are not there to those with normal sight and perception).

I am a spiritual person. Christianity is the foundation of my beliefs, though none of the religious traditions would seem to have an exclusive path to one having a meaningful and rewarding relationship to God and the whole of our lives and eternity. We all are one. As you grow into the spiritual world and receive the knowing and insights beyond yourself and your self-imposed bounds, accept that it is real.

Let me tell you about my late husband, Gary. Although I live with my daughter and son-in-law, I live independently in a ground-level lakefront self-contained "mother-in-law" part of their house. I have two bedrooms, a full bathroom, a kitchen, and a living room. I came to live with them because I lost my dear sweet husband, Gary, in a traffic accident in 2009, the same year I lost my sight. Gary is a huge bump in the night for me.

I remember the denial, confusion, and frustration I had when I started losing my sight. Then it got to the point where I just couldn't deny it anymore; I was going blind. I couldn't see well enough to put my eyebrows on anymore. I became more and more dependent on Gary. "Will you open this?" "Will you read this for me?" "Will you help set the dryer properly?" "Will you dial Cheryl's phone number?" "Turn the car around; I forgot my sunglasses. The bright sun hurts my eyes." On and on, every little thing I needed, I needed assistance with. I ended up making demands just to function.

I wore him down, and it was showing. Our marriage was changing; nothing was fun any longer. We were losing what Gary and I had most of all, and that was fun with one another. Gary started doing the grocery shopping and the house chores. He even started eating out because I no longer wanted to cook. I just wanted to stay in bed with my head under a pillow. Our marriage was going from one of partnership to one of a caregiver in a lopsided marriage.

It was only through his solid support and optimistic attitude that I got through my crisis at all. One time I was trying to plug the vacuum into those little friggin' electrical holes and couldn't find them. I was crying, and Gary came over and gently took the cord from me and plugged it in. Then he wrapped his big arms around me, held me tight, and said, "Everything will be okay, honey. We'll make it through this together."

Gary finally took me by the hand and dragged me to SAAVI. I went in with both feet dug into the ground, saying, "No! No! No!" I did not go in willingly. I wasn't a child who had to go to school to learn; I was an adult. Blind school! No! Who would want to be with a bunch of people bumping into each other and dogs sniffing at you in the wrong places?

SAAVI school turned out to be the best thing that could have happened to me. I stayed an extra six months, and when they said I had learned all that they could teach me, I joined the alumni just so I could still hang out and continue participating in classes.

I found my gift was helping newcomers to dump their garbage and to cry. Then, after they were able to let those thoughts go, I helped them recycle those thoughts by encouraging constructive learning and habits.

My current bump in the night is gone in body but not in spirit. Often, I see ghosts from out of the corner of my eye. I'm not sure if I am nuts, but I know I'm not afraid. I even talk to them. It's a phenomenon for people with low vision. They often see glimpses of things and people from the past. Maybe it's a flicker of a memory presenting itself. It might be a glimpse, a living memory, or a connection from meditation and sleep.

Recently I awoke exactly at midnight (remember my talking clocks) and saw Gary standing inside my window. My smart speaker started playing country western music (Gary's favorite), seemingly from out of the blue. I came out to my front room to see if someone was there asking the smart speaker to play the music. No one was there, and when I went back into my room, Gary was gone, but I am reassured he is here, close with me in my graying world.

My aunt Helen comes to me often, in memory if not in spirit. She was a great influence back in my high school days. My family moved from a small town in Wisconsin to California. It was a true awaking for a Midwest girl to move all the way to the coast of California. I moved to Marin County, which is just across the Golden Gate Bridge from the great city of San Francisco. San Francisco was considered the city of all cities at the time—the "City on the Seven Hills," the "City by the Bay." It was a very cosmopolitan city in 1954. Women would never be seen walking the downtown streets of San Francisco without their hats and gloves and perhaps fox stoles wrapped around their shoulders. Men were dapper in their suits, ties, and hats. Such was Aunt Helen's life.

My daddy was going to work for Aunt Helen and her husband, Uncle Don. They owned a couple of apartment tower buildings, and they had just purchased a new dental business, which my daddy would help them with. They were very rich.

I was going to be a senior in a new high school. What a culture shock. My aunt Helen took one look at me and said, "Oh my God, we'll have to go shopping." I didn't understand. Didn't everyone wear jeans with the legs rolled up to two inches below their knees and their father's' old white shirts with the sleeves rolled up? Well, no, not according to Aunt Helen and California living. So, four new poodle skirts, four new cashmere sweaters, a pair of white gloves, a pair of brown and white saddle shoes, and a new pillbox hat completed my transformation. She finished me off with a new haircut from Elizabeth Arden's.

Just before my first day of school, Aunt Helen asked, "How are you getting to school?" Since I hadn't planned anything, she promptly went and got her car keys and handed them to me. They were keys to a yellow Pontiac Chieftain convertible. By the end of the first day of school, I had a whole car full of girls riding with me, showing me all the make-out spots. I became a popular girl, more popular than I ever expected. I even made the cheerleading squad and was elected head cheerleader. What an influence Aunt Helen had on me growing up. She would later be an influence on my daughters.

We only stayed in California one year and then returned to Wisconsin. I was determined to return to California. As a single mother, I did return in the early 1960s with my young daughter. Our new life found me as a straight-commissioned advertising salesperson, one of the few women at that time working full time in sales, calling on San Francisco businesspeople. I could write a book about my sales life in the big city, but I will save that for another time.

As we do sometimes, we can put things together when we look back. I remember that Helen was always looking for her glasses. She wore those big thick green Mr. Magoo Coke bottle glasses, ones that made the wearer's eyes look distorted and funny. Even with the glasses, she was always saying, "I can't see; I can't see anything anymore." As young people will, my daughter and I tended to ignore her complaints and sometimes even become irritated when sent to find her glasses once again.

Once while talking with Aunt Helen on the back porch, she remarked how beautiful and full the moon was. My little unfiltered daughter said that maybe it was Aunty Helen's cocktail talking again, and she giggled. What Helen thought was the moon was a streetlight shining over her shoulder. I only remembered this because years later a similar thing happened to me. Oh, genetics, you got me. In Aunt Helen's day, many people complained of low vision, but it wasn't until recently that they have put a name to the disease.

Reflecting back, maybe I should have shown a lot more sympathy. I sure wish I could tell her that I understand and know what she meant. Without a doubt, Aunt Helen's bump in the night now guides me through turmoil or indecision.

I loved California, and California loved me. Thank you, Aunt Helen, and may you always rest in peace. All that's left are all the thoughts and dreams that go through my head as dreams, apparitions, memories, or even illusions. All of those memory bumps make us who we are. These are patterns for our speech, behavior, and attitude toward life—and of course our sense of humor. I do not allow my thoughts to give devils, dreams, or any type of monster the opportunity to be in my life. If I give them fear or even recognize them, the thoughts take on life. So, I don't believe in them. Of course, there is evil, but I avoid those thoughts. Fear can paralyze you. How can we believe in a loving God and fear too?

Because of our sight loss, it seems all of our other senses heighten— smell certainly, hearing too. We can feel energy lightly brushing our skin receptors, surrounding us with the vibrations of life. So, when they say low-vision people see ghosts and things that others can't, maybe they are right.

Still today, eleven years later, Gary will come to me in the middle of the night just to let me know he is there and loves me. Maybe, just maybe, we can see deeper and clearer than sighted people. When you say the word *ghost*, people want to creep out, but usually these spirits are people that loved us, like our moms, dads, husband or wives, brothers or sisters, or close friends. It could even be the family pet, like my dog Mitzie, a fifteen-pound black poodle who was with me for fifteen years and is still with me on the kitchen floor or at the bottom of the bed. I often try to figure out how a spirit could come to us. Do they travel to us through dimensions? What do they do to materialize to us? Is it because we are unsighted that we can illuminate them? Is that the reason we are more receptive? Is it possible the ghosts come to guide us, to comfort us? It is my belief that all caretakers, dead or alive, will help us now that we cannot see clearly anymore. You pick your belief. I choose to believe it is God's protection.

Bumps in the night can be used as a time of silence, of praying and meditation. It probably takes concentration and practice to learn to smell the flowers and just be silent. I have a special little saying to create my visions, my reality, and have calm and silence. Bless my bumps in the night.

Hearing and Touch

As a special gift, I can hear water beginning to boil on the stove, or know if the dog wants in, or hear every little sound around me that I choose to.

Hearing is protection for us, especially outside near traffic. Listen and listen.

As for touch, feel everything unless it moves or bites. Remember, upon entering a new area, not only can you touch with your fingers but with your feet as well. Know when you have left tile and are now on carpeting or maybe even grass, for instance. Feel with your feet. Stepping from a curb onto blacktop is a completely different touch with your feet.

Touching and hearing has become my guide for life. We touch our children, our beloved pets, everything in our world. Don't forget to give yourself a hug. Have courage and know you're not alone. Your higher power is holding your hand and guiding you with every step you take.

It is known that when you lose one of your senses, the others heighten. I have found that I can hear extremely well. Loud noises, like the ringing of bells, may make me jump. I try to avoid loud sirens, slamming doors, and high-pitched bells.

Touch is what gives me a great big smile and is what I call swimming through the house. Breezes should be noticed at doorways. I touch cupboard tops, door handles, and corners of the wall as I glide from room to room. I have become very familiar with the way to the bathroom on a midnight run. When I am back in the doorway of my bedroom, I take two steps in, turn right, take two steps, turn left, take three steps and my knees hit the mattress, all for my safe return back to sleep and dreamland. Feel with your feet when going from room to room. Count your steps. Be "touchy-feely."

Hearing and feeling the atmosphere in rooms will make me jump and even cause my body to shake. The sharp high-pitched sounds seem to penetrate my very being.

I just want to say one more thing about hearing and touch. I am so grateful that most of my life I was sighted so that I can know what, where, and how life and the world work. It is a real opportunity to learn new ways.

HUMOR

Make yourself challenge yourself and find new ways to make yourself and those around you laugh and have fun. Brighten everyone's day. Be normal—but then, what's normal?

We all have a story to tell, and the world needs your strength and hope. Nobody cares to hear negativity of the past. They need to hear what you have learned in this life and how you have grown. Whenever we are not growing, we are dying. We were not born to die—we were born to live, love and laugh.

Since the beginning of time, cavemen communicated with their grunts and groans. How we communicate is such an important part of our life. Just because we are visually impaired does not mean we must sit in a corner and wilt. We need to begin. Just begin.

We need to be creative and laugh a lot. When in doubt, laugh. We must change our attitude and go forward with a vision to have a blessed day.

Avoid negative ideas and topics. I avoid "the four D's" for a starter: death, disease, divorce, and disaster. Other taboo topics become obvious when you remember this advice. Always laugh with people, not at them or others.

In order to change the world, it's time to help our fellow beings who are struggling in various ways. Ask yourself, "What have I learned and how have I grown?"

These are the stories the world needs to hear.

SEX

Everyone says I have to have some sex in the book in order for it to sell, so here it is.

Take off your glasses and do it.

WALKING TALL

Many of us tend to look down at our feet while walking, fearing that we will run into obstacles. Instead, stand tall, with chin up, and keep your eyes looking forward. Looking five to six feet ahead works well for me.

Even today, I remember walking by my grandma as a young girl, hearing grandma say, "Pull those shoulders back. Stand straight; hold your head up high. Tuck that butt in; suck that stomach in." Finally, she would say, "Eyes forward." We even practiced walking around the house with a book balanced on the tops of our heads. I was told that was what the movie stars did for good posture. Present yourself like the shiny star you are. You just need to be proud of who you are.

Leading techniques are a matter of choice. The correct way to lead a visually impaired person is to have the sighted leader walk with one arm across their rib section, while the person being led grabs their elbow lightly. This way if the leader falls, they go down alone, and vice versa. Personally, I like to take the chance and hold hands with my leader.

Then I can feel whether the person's energy is high or low, warm and fuzzy or grumpy, and I can act accordingly.

Recently I discovered a great new way to be led. My daughter and I were walking along a hallway, and she was carrying a folded-up umbrella for the pending rain. I offered to carry it, but she only let go of one end and I held the other and we just tracked along perfectly. We were able to move rapidly but with great balance. Any short baton, small umbrella, stick, or folded-up cane should work.

One of my challenges is walking through a doorway without knocking my elbow on the jamb. When being led, the sighted person should drop their arm and extend back their hand, essentially pulling you safely through the doorway. In self-closing doorways, there's always confusion. They try to hold the door open with their butt, while I try not to bash my elbows or trip over the doorjamb. Try it. When you figure it out, let me know.

In the meantime, show your pride and show self-confidence. Keep your head held up high, shoulders back. Walk tall and be the star you are.

I Remember When

I remember when I realized I should write this book to share what I have learned about coping with my low vision. I remember that I could see a little better then but know that I feel better now.

I remember the iceman with his horse-drawn trailer coming through our neighborhood and delivering big hunks of ice for all the houses that could afford iceboxes. He chipped off chunks of ice for all the neighborhood kids running after him for an icy.

I remember sunrises and sunsets clearly.

I remember taking three clotheslines and hanging a bedsheet spread open so we could hang our panties, bras, and nightgowns out of sight of the neighbors.

I remember my first kiss; it was in my mom's fruit cellar. His name was Jimmy Coleman. I hid from my mom's eyes for days because I just knew she would know I had been kissed on the lips.

I remember big Saturday morning chores so I could earn twelve cents for watching the matinee that afternoon.

I remember seeing my brother, who I always had to take everywhere, steal a candy bar at the movie, and I told my dad. Wow, what a deal. He reminded me of the consequences seventy years later.

I remember my grandmother's street address and telephone number.

I remember seeing Elvis Presley's first appearance on television. It was on *The Ed Sullivan Show*. Elvis was not allowed to gyrate or wiggle at all. I remember my mother saying to me, "He will be a big star."

I remember bubble gum wrapped with a comic on the wrapping paper.

I remember my oldest daughter's daddy saying repeatedly, "Your beautiful eyes, your beautiful eyes."

I remember dressing up every Halloween. We children had to go to the old folks' home and give out orange napkins filled with treats. After that was done, we were turned loose to trick or treat.

I remember President Kennedy being shot and all the outrage when the first Catholic president was to be elected. The worries were that the pope was going to take over the United States.

I remember watching *Fibber Magee and Molly, Jimmy Durante, Gunsmoke, Tales of Wells Fargo, The $64,000 Question, Captain Kangaroo* and *The Liberace Show.*

I remember the bombing of Pearl Harbor, and I didn't know where that was. I knew it was terrible because my mom and dad had just purchased the Sugar Bowl, a high school hangout in Stevens Point, Wisconsin. All the students were coming to my mom and dad to say goodbye as we were watching them leave for the war. My mom was crying a lot.

I remember my grandmother, who only had three daughters, telling me, "If I had had a son, I would wish he would have been just like your father."

I remember that I could read the baking instructions for a chocolate cake mix.

I remember my baby girl being delivered into my arms for the very first time.

I remember when my father came into my room as my mom was dressing me in a bright red formal that she had made. My dad said, "I can see you will be the most beautiful girl at the senior prom. You look just like your mother."

I remember when I could see.

I remember when I tried to buy a house and was told by the bank, "No, you're single, self-employed, and on a straight-commission income. Beside you're a woman and might get pregnant." Thanks to a smart real estate person, I purchased a home for my two daughters and me on a land contract. I spent years in real estate helping first-time buyers, both single men and women. You just never know when your life will change because of one of life's learning lessons. Carry on.

I can remember when at the Sugar Bowl (again, a high school hangout) I could order a banana split with three scoops of different ice cream and three requested toppings and a cherry on top—for twenty-five cents.

The very first homemade ice cream, pinball, and jukebox in Stevens Point, Wisconsin, were there. This would be around 1950. My parents, Clark and Lenore Lampe, owned the Sugar Bowl.

I remember when I thought becoming and finally being visually impaired was the biggest curse or most horrible thing that could happen to a person.

Today I am most grateful for this disability because I have met so many new wonderful people going through the same thing. We give each other positive thoughts and lots of love and compassion. Most of all, I'm grateful for meeting you and offering you this book. I am so glad I can share some of my life with you and offer some tips and tricks for the visually impaired. I hope we can all say together, "I remember when I [meaning you] decided to create a new life and maybe even laugh at some of the dumb things we can do." I hope you will reach out to me and share your "remember whens."

Printed in the United States
By Bookmasters